"*Safe in the Arms of Love* offers music that is tender for the hearts, ears and spirits of newborn listeners. These delicate musical invitations soothe parent, child and caregiver."

DON CAMPBELL, Author, *The Mozart Effect® for Children,* **Director, Aesthetic Audio Systems**

"From hospital to home, this music should be in every newborn environment. *Safe in the Arms of Love* establishes a musical sanctuary for that which is truly important—meaningful contact and connection. Beautifully melding artistry with scientifically proven principles, Lisa Rafel and Gary Malkin have produced music that can be easily absorbed by the nervous systems of all. The effect will last long beyond the music."

JOSHUA LEEDS, Author, *The Power Of Sound; Through A Dog's Ear,* **Director, Essential Sounds**

"*Safe in the Arms of Love* delivers on every level. It has warmth, exquisite arrangements—a work of true beauty. It's the perfect baby shower gift or truly a gift for anyone. The love just shines through."

ELLEN F. FRANKLIN, Co-author, *Acutonics From Galaxies to Cells; Planetary Science, Harmony and Medicine,* **CEO, Kairos Institute of Sound Healing, LLC**

"This ground-breaking work will be a cherished treasure for the whole family. The nurturing voices with rich accompaniment will hold you and your baby in the arms of love."

CHRISTINA TOURIN, Author, *Cradle of Sound,* **Director, International Harp Therapy Program**

"Although I know the music is intended for nursing mothers to assist with bonding—a purpose that I am confident it will fulfill—I also experience it as helpful for people of all ages to open their heart and reconnect with their gentleness. After all, who among us doesn't carry wounds that cannot benefit from a good dose of love and tenderness?"

TIM WEITZEL PH. D., Dynamic Learning Systems

"Lisa Rafel and company have delighted us with a gift that is beautiful, precious and tender. Each musical piece flows into the next and is reminiscent of the comfort and love of my grandmother's quilts. My newborn loves the CD and it acts as her pacifier."

MAESTRO CURTIS, Composer

"As every parent recognizes, there is an innate sense of rhythm in every child. The constantly varying rhythms of heartbeat and breath, tuned to mom's emotions, supply a rich, 24/7 symphony in the womb. To no one's surprise, research has shown a powerful impact of music on mood and the physiology of the human heart. Listening to *Safe in the Arms of Love*, I am profoundly reminded of the importance of protecting the sacred bond between newborn and mother, and providing music to complement an experience that will influence the course of a lifetime. This music is beautiful, gently uplifting and peaceful, and perfectly sets the mood for mother and baby to bond in a relaxed and emotionally supportive environment."

STEVEN F. HOROWITZ, M.D., Chief of Cardiology, Stamford Hospital, and Director of Integrative Cardiology, The Center for Health and Wellness

"As both a psychiatrist and mother, I can attest to the critical importance of healthy bonding. If you are a new parent, or about to be a new parent, drop everything and experience the beauty and impact of *Safe in the Arms of Love*. This is great music to support the bonding process and deepen the relationship between parents and newborn."

HYLA CASS, M.D., Author, *Eight Weeks to Vibrant Health*

"When certain music is added to the chaotic newborn environment, it can become a "settling embrace," bringing a calming message of hope and self-confidence. *Safe in the Arms of Love* fills the gap many new parents experience of not having their mothers to help and advise them during this important transition. As a new grandmother, if I were unable to be there for my son and his wife, I would hope that someone would put *Safe in the Arms of Love* into their hands. It is nothing short of magical."

BETHANY HAYS, M.D., OB-GYN and Functional Medicine

"Every once in a while, a new body of work comes along that jumps beyond what has been done before. *Safe in the Arms of Love* is a powerful, tender and heart-opening mix of songs and music that moves the parent and cradles the child. In my work with men, this music has become a valuable tool in connecting them to their experience as a father as well as to their own inner child."

STEPHEN JOHNSON, Ph.D., Clinical Psychologist, Director, Los Angeles Men's Center

"As a mother who nursed four children and being a therapeutic musician myself, I love the ebb and flow of this recording, and I can easily imagine a mom and baby being drawn ever more deeply into peaceful connection. I was deeply touched by the tenderness of Lisa Rafel's songs and the expressiveness of the singers' performances."

MELINDA GARDINER, RN, CMP, Executive Director, Music for Healing and Transition Program, Inc.

"As a therapist working with children of all ages with their families, I have found that *Safe in the Arms of Love* creates a soothing sound environment that contributes to the connection of heart energies. Each song is an invitation to relax and engage. Listening to several songs in succession has helped to bring a foundation of peace to our clinical sessions. One mother, having witnessed the breathing, heart rate, behavior, and engagement changes in her infant son during a treatment session in which we were using this CD, remarked that she wouldn't have believed it if she hadn't seen it for herself! *Safe in the Arms of Love* is a valued addition to my sound/music resources and a frequent recommendation to parents."

SHEILA ALLEN, MA, OTR, BCP, Co-Director and Co-Founder of Pediatric Therapeutics

"The songs of *Safe in the Arms of Love* were originally written for nursing mothers and babies. However, as I walked and rocked my grandson to this music it touched my grandmother's heart as well. The music is relaxing and reassuring on a deep emotional level. Late at night I often play this lovely music. I find the music very calming and my strong family values are supported and expressed by these wise and wonderful lyrics. We can all feel safely 'in the arms of love' just by listening to these sweet songs."

LINDA AVERY, Physical Therapist, Childbirth Educator

"As I listen to *Safe in the Arms of Love*, it opens up very deep and early connections to my vulnerability and sensitivity, creating many possibilities for healing. One that seems clear to me is the healing of the very early loss of the feeling of being held, cherished, and safe. This experience is not only healing for wounds of early childhood, but makes it possible to be more open to perceiving the deeper aspects of essential nature, and to joyfully connect with that experience. What if we could live each day in touch with not only life in the physical world, but also in connection with Spirit life? What a gift this music is!"

REGINA REILLY, M.S., Marriage Family Therapist for over 30 years, Teacher of the Diamond Approach

"*Safe in the Arms of Love* makes you feel as if you are in the midst of your very own fairy tale! These universal songs awaken an ancient knowing, reminding you that your baby is a gift from Grace, lovingly supported by our ancestors. Like a prayer set to music, you can actually use this music to heal the alienation that can so often result from not having your own early bonding experience. Unlike most books in this genre, it elegantly affirms the importance of the father's role in the bonding process and will help young fathers deepen their loving relationship with their children. *Safe in the Arms of Love* is a perfect gift for anyone expecting a child."

LUISAH TEISH, Master storyteller, teacher and ritualist, Author, *Jambalaya: The Natural Woman's Book of Personal Charms and Practical Rituals*

Safe *in the* Arms *of* Love

Safe *in the* Arms *of* Love

DEEPENING THE ESSENTIAL BOND WITH YOUR BABY

BY
Lisa Rafel, Gary Malkin, and David Surrenda, Ph.D.

FEATURING ORIGINAL SONGS BY
Lisa Rafel

MUSIC PRODUCED AND ARRANGED BY
Gary Malkin

FOREWORD BY
Christiane Northrup, M.D.
Author, *Women's Bodies, Women's Wisdom*

A MESSAGE FROM
Marshall Klaus, M.D., Phyllis Klaus, MFT, LMSW
Authors, *Your Amazing Newborn, Bonding,* and *The Doula Book*

AFTERWORD BY
Joel Evans, M.D.
Author, *The Whole Pregnancy Handbook*

ALSO BY LISA RAFEL

It Began in Kathmandu (Book of Poetry and Photographs)

Ancient Prayers of Alia (CD)

Soul Songs of the Labyrinth (CD)

Space/Time Phenomena (CD)

Precious Life (CD)

ALSO BY GARY MALKIN

Graceful Passages: A Companion for Living and Dying
(co-produced by Michael Stillwater) Book and 2 CD set

Grace in Practice: A Clinical Application Guide for Graceful Passages

Unspeakable Grace: The Music of Graceful Passages

*Care for the Journey: Music and Messages for Sustaining the Heart
of Healthcare* (co-produced by Michael Stillwater) (CD)

Healing your Life after the Loss of a Loved One (CD)

The Heart of Healing: Music and Messages for the Healing Journey (CD)

The Exhale Series: Piano Improvisations for Healing Environments (CD Series)

The Music of the Great Smoky Mountains (CD)

Thousand Pieces of Gold (CD)

The Calling: Songs from the Heart (CD)

ALSO BY DAVID S. SURRENDA, Ph.D.

Retooling on the Run (with Stuart Heller)

Domestic Crisis Intervention (with Jeffrey Schwartz)

Correctional Crisis Intervention (with Jeffrey Schwartz)

Dedication

FROM LISA

To my dear grandparents, Sophie and Elias Jerome,
who loved me fiercely, gently, joyfully and unconditionally.
They are the source from which my words flow.

FROM DAVID

To my mother, Blanche, and my grandmother Pauline,
who generously gave me the essential ingredients of
healthy bonding—their love and special care.

FROM GARY

To my mother and father, Pearl and Irving Malkin,
who always demonstrated unconditional love,
helping me to understand parenting as the greatest
privilege I will ever experience.

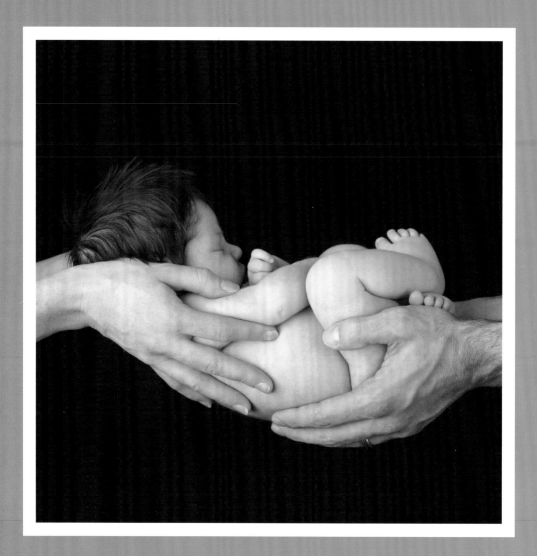

Table of Contents

Welcome

This is a gift just for you—

A place where
words and music can open your heart
Where tenderness and beauty can ease your mind.

This is the time to be with your baby
soul to soul . . .
and it all happens because of you!

Foreword by
Christiane Northrup, M.D.

*T*HE PROCESS OF BONDING WITH A NEW BABY IMPRINTS A CHILD'S sense of safety and security in the world—as well as a sense of belonging. This imprint has lifelong consequences for the quality of one's immunity and overall health. If a child feels that all is well, that she is loved, and that there will be enough of what she needs, then her immunity is much more likely to flourish.

Safe in the Arms of Love is a practical and powerful way to use the power of music to help facilitate a positive bonding experience with your baby. These songs go right to the heart, allowing you to relax, open up, and find an oasis of calm in your daily routine—an oasis which will help you and your baby flourish. Listen to these songs while you nurse or at bedtime. And make them a regular part of your baby care routine. Your heart—and your baby, will thank you.

> If a child feels that all is well, that she is loved, and that there will be enough of what she needs, then her immunity is much more likely to flourish.

Christiane Northrup, M.D.
Author, *Women's Bodies, Women's Wisdom* and *Mother-Daughter Wisdom*

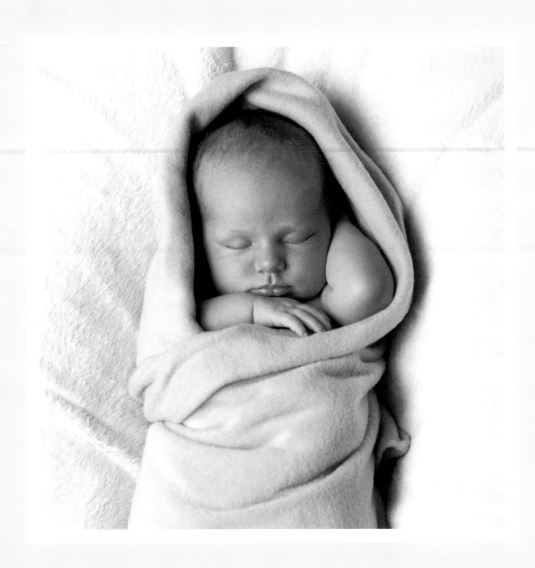

SAFE IN THE ARMS OF LOVE IS A SPECIAL PACKAGE OF BEAUTIFUL music, especially created, sung, and arranged to elicit feelings of calm and love. The tender words of the lyrics serve to enhance the deep bond between parent and child in this early period. The thoughtful book describes the parent-child relationship sensitively, recognizing and addressing the steps parents can take to naturally and joyfully bond. It presents helpful understanding that reflects the past half-century of work in the area of bonding.

In the first hours and days of life, babies have the capacity to interact with their close relatives. Right from the beginning the baby can see its mother's and father's face, can respond to their parents' touch and remember their voices from uterine life. In addition, newborns can remember the music they heard played repeatedly when in the uterus and will often respond after birth by quieting and listening with interest.

Because infants cannot regulate themselves, a major goal of parents is to soothe and calm their baby, especially if the baby is in distress. To return to calm, babies require sensitive and responsive caregivers. The calming and comforting effects of Lisa Rafel's music and Gary Malkin's arrangements can aid this process. While soothing their baby, the parents benefit by being immersed in these healing sounds. The gentle resonance evoked by this music can help in the development of a secure attachment that will benefit the baby throughout his or her life.

Marshall Klaus, M.D., Phyllis Klaus, MFT, LMSW
Authors, *Your Amazing Newborn*, *Bonding*, and *The Doula Book*

Introduction

LISA RAFEL

*O*NE DAY MY HUSBAND AND I WERE WALKING IN A STORE WHEN a new mother stopped nearby with her baby in a stroller. My husband stopped talking and turned to the little one. He said, "ba ba ba." The baby's eyes opened wide and then they both smiled.

Since that day, I make it a point to stop what I am doing to say hello to a baby. I like to say, "Welcome! We are so glad that you are here! Thank you for coming." The parent usually smiles as the baby looks at me with such wide eyes and seems to know what I am saying.

How should we be with these new beings?

When your baby leaves the safety and relative serenity of the womb, she enters a dramatically different world. It is critical for her to experience a transition that maintains an intimate connection to her mother and father and to all those loving arms that will care for her. *Safe in the Arms of Love* provides an opportunity to fulfill every parent's wish to have a deep and heartfelt connection with their child.

When you become a parent, you too make a transition as you cross a threshold into a whole new way of being. The environment you create is what nourishes and stimulates your baby to learn and grow. Initially, this transition can be difficult.

> Welcome! We are so glad that you are here! Thank you for coming.

You quickly discover that time is no longer your own. Your attention can get scattered. You will probably find yourself feeling very tired from the lack of

How do you create time for intimate connection with your baby?

sleep. There is so much to do. Your many responsibilities seem to carve away any personal time.

*J*uggling all of this can be daunting. There are endless chores, phone calls, and interruptions in the midst of essential responsibilities that must be met, especially by working and single parents. Even when you have help, managing this change can be overwhelming without the proper support and tools. So how do you create time for intimate connection with your baby? Often that can occur in the early morning or late at night, but the lack of sleep can make it difficult to settle down. The baby can get fussy and you might get frustrated. Learning to stay open-hearted and calm is the key.

Safe in the Arms of Love is a musical resource that fosters a loving, uninterrupted connection between you and your baby. The CD consists of songs and interludes to support a calm and heartfelt experience. The songs contain psycho-acoustically designed music with evocative words to touch your heart. Psycho-acoustically designed music intentionally uses rhythm, tone and tempo to create a specific effect. The songs

in *Safe in the Arms of Love* utilize these principles to ensure that your listening experience is relaxing and enjoyable. The instrumental interludes allow you to slow down and feel the relationship between you and your baby. As you do this, you can create your own way of talking, singing, and being with her. Let this time inspire you to share your own loving words in celebration of your child.

Safe in the Arms of Love provides a peaceful refuge from the stresses of every day life. Let your friends and family know that listening to the CD is a special time you are devoting to being with your baby. Let the phone go to voicemail. Turn the TV off. You can also use the music to assist you if you feel a little down or overwhelmed. If your child is colicky or cannot be soothed, the music can help support your capacities for patience and understanding. It will help to de-stress your breathing, open your heart and reawaken you to the wonder of being with your baby, whether you're nursing, putting your child to sleep, or simply needing "down" time.

If you listen to this music while your baby is still in the womb, she will recognize the music after she is born! Playing the CD for the baby's siblings, grandparents and other family members can initiate a powerful bonding process for the whole family. This provides a great way to share the love as you look forward to your baby being born.

*R*educing stress and providing interactive, loving attention to your prenatal or newborn baby is critical for their healthy foundation. We hope that you will use *Safe in the Arms of Love* on a regular basis. It can provide the inspiration and renewal you need to maintain an openhearted experience during the precious and critical early days of your baby's life. A sustained, intimate connection will create a deep and enduring bond between you and your child. Spending this time together will be among the most important and satisfying things you will ever do.

Dr. David says:

THE ESSENCE OF RELATIONSHIP IS COMMUNICATION

Infants begin their lives by communicating through their senses. The infant experiences touch, smell, sound, and proximity. While in the womb, the baby lived within a protected environment of gentle movement, sensation and sound. Out of the womb, everything is intensified—new feelings, new sounds, new sights, new smells, and new textures. The one constant for the infant is the connection to its parents. How that connection is experienced is the key to healthy bonding and a healthy beginning of life.

A baby knows its parents through recognizing the familiar sound of the voice and the reassuring beat of the heart. When a newborn experiences the sensory connections of touch, smell and sensation in a positive way, safety and trust are natural consequences.

Bonding is about having a "place in the world" within the context of family and community. It is a connection to the core of our shared humanity, being a part of the larger human family as well our personal family. Without successful bonding, we might forever strive to know ourselves in relationship. With the right early experiences, the bond that is created is lifelong.

Prelude

The sounds sprinkle down, down, down,
into the skin, through the skin,
into the water that surrounds a little soul.
The sounds enter the little ears so newly formed,
still swimming in the liquid of life.
Beat, beat goes the mother's heart;
Swoosh, swoosh, the sounds come and go;
This is the music of you—
a symphony in swirling tides—
Bathing each fiber of this new and precious life.

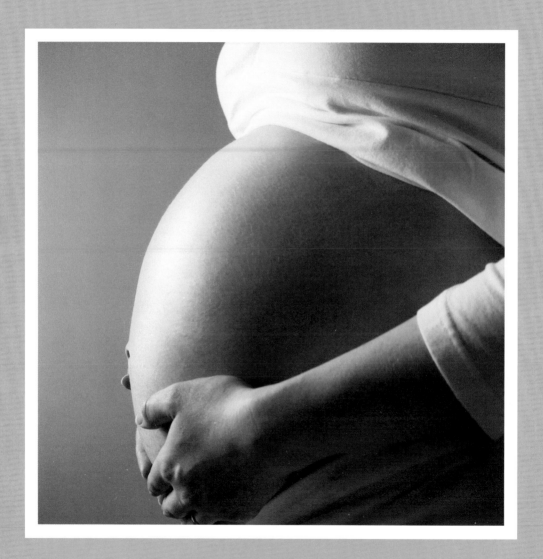

Your Baby Is Listening

LISA RAFEL

EVEN IN THE WOMB, YOUR BABY IS LISTENING.

*I*MAGINE BEAUTIFUL MUSIC FILTERING INTO THE REMARKABLE world of your womb. As the musical vibrations enter like a soft breeze, they caress your baby's little body and newly formed skin. The frequencies of the notes encounter your baby's tiny nervous system and stimulate her multiplying cells.

Your own loving words are like beautiful music. Their sounds are vibrations that your baby can feel. Transmitted through the mother's tissues, bones and fluids, they establish the tone for how your baby knows you. He can recognize that you are his mother or father through the sound of your voice.

Though your baby is able to hear from its ninth week of gestation, and has fully developed ears by four and a half months, it is not only through his ears that he receives the vibration of tone and sound. Once his nervous system forms, his body experiences a feeling/hearing state similar to the sympathetic resonance that occurs when frequencies vibrate in relationship with each other. For example, if an "A" string on a guitar is plucked, the "A" string on any nearby guitar will also vibrate sympathetically, making the same sound even though it was not plucked.

> The sounds of your words become vibrations that your baby can feel.

In a similar way, what a mother is feeling in her body impacts her baby in the womb. The mother and child have been attuning to each other from the baby's initial capacity to feel. This happens in two ways. First, the mother's emotional

How you connect with your baby establishes the foundation for their capacity for empathy, love, learning and compassion.

state is transmitted to the baby through shared body chemistry. Feelings are communicated through words, sounds and emotions. Second, the baby is affected by the sounds it hears, including internal sounds from the mother, and external sounds that penetrate the mother's skin. No matter who is caring for the child, this attunement can occur through the sounds of a loving voice speaking directly through the skin.

You can create a sympathetic, Positive Emotional Resonance (PER) between you and your developing baby by how you speak and sing to him. He can increasingly identify your voice and respond to your words as he matures. Medical research has shown that during labor some babies respond to their mother's communication and move or turn to assist in their delivery.

ONCE YOUR BABY ENTERS THIS WORLD

*Y*our baby is highly sensitive to external stimulation. In those first moments though his eyes cannot see clearly, he can hear and feel your voice, even with the new light and all the sounds happening around him. The out-of-womb environment can be over-whelming. Many cultures believe special care is needed during a baby's transition from the womb to the world. In some indigenous cultures the baby stays in a darkened room for a specific number of days, often lying skin to skin on its parent's chest. With heart on heart, the transition from the inner to the outer world becomes a gentle, loving and connecting transition time for parents and baby. "Heart songs" may be sung during that time. Babies love heart-felt songs, particularly if they have an easy melody, a repetitive pattern and are attuned to the rhythm of the human heart.

*y*our newborn baby's brain and nervous system start soaking up stimuli at an astonishing rate. At birth, your baby has one billion neurons, or brain cells. Each neuron forms up to 15,000 separate connections. This means your baby has more synaptic connections than all the stars in the universe!

A parent who thoughtfully manages and enhances the baby's stimulation sets the environmental tone and influences how he grows and learns.

Touch and sound, which includes voice and music, are the most effective ways to communicate with your baby's nervous system. Gently touching and massaging your baby establishes an important chemical connection that instills a sense of calm and well-being. When you sing gently with repeating patterns and speak in a soft, loving sing-song voice, the sound is soothing to both of you and supports the growing bond between you.

Dr. David says:

PRENATAL IMPACT OF MUSIC

Research studies over the past 25 years point to the power of sound as an influence on prenatal infants. Studies suggest that babies in the womb are sensitive, responsive, and learning oriented. These studies reveal the power of music to impact prenatal memory, responsiveness and health. Babies who hear music in utero do have a memory and preference for the music to which they were exposed.

MEMORY AND PREFERENCE

A Newborns learn and remember their mother's heartbeat and voice.

B Newborns prefer the music they heard their mother sing while in utero rather than new material sung by their mother.

C Babies "remember" music they heard in utero and prefer it to new music.

D In utero infants prefer tempos that resemble their own heart beat.

E Babies prefer hearing those stories, music, rhymes and poems heard initially in the womb.

IMPLICATIONS

1 As a parent, the sounds you make, your sonic environment and the sounds your baby hears in utero are vitally important and impact your baby.

2 Using sound to deliberately create the right environment is an important step in mindful parenting.

3 Music can be a great way to initiate the bonding process with your in utero baby.

The Essential Bond

DAVID SURRENDA, PH.D.

EVERY CULTURE BONDS!

THE DESIRE TO CONNECT IS UNIVERSAL. ALL OVER THE WORLD we can see that people interact with babies in a unique way. There is a reason so many people speak in "baby talk" and act playfully with a baby. It's because it is an experience that makes us feel good and babies really like it. You can see it in their eyes and in the way they laugh and smile. When the connection is heartfelt, intimacy and trust grow in the baby and protective instincts grow in the parents. For the mother, this primal connection is called bonding and for the baby, it is called attachment.

EVERY CHILD NEEDS TO BOND

The infant-parent bond is fundamental to all future relationship success. Forming and nurturing strong connections between parents and their children is critical because what babies learn in their first interactions is central to becoming a healthy person. In essence, an appropriate attachment shapes how the child's personality grows and develops.

> Connection is the first thing every human being experiences.

It has been proven that during the first hours after birth there is a special opportunity for deep bonding to occur between mother and child.

*R*esearch by child development experts, neuroscientists and psychologists has consistently shown that early experiences with mother and father influence the child's brain and eventually their capacity to live an emotionally healthy life. The infant's ability and confidence to cope and survive in the world is directly shaped by the baby-parent relationship.

onding is the ground of human experience where we discover and explore what it means to relate. The first thing every human being experiences is connection. It is the point of beginning, the unfolding from one's original cellular self. If this connection evolves, as it should, it becomes as natural as breathing. If this connection isn't properly formed, it can feel like being lost in space, without directions to guide you.

Bonding forms a foundation of trust through which we come to know the world. The remarkable mix of feeding, holding, nurturing and speaking to the baby creates the special connection we call birth bonding. Nursing, and the physical sensations that accompany it, are deeply intimate. Through the powerful experience of nursing and the warm touch that accompanies it, the baby is nourished and satisfied.

For the biological mother, the physiological process between mother and child is a profound experience. They share the same space, the same body, and the same blood. Pregnancy is also a deeply psychological experience for the mother. When she says "yes" in her whole being, it initiates the natural process of bonding. This potent, primal connection can be developed from nurturing physical contact that utilizes the five essential ways of bonding even when the mother is an adoptive parent, or using a surrogate.

Of all the music that reaches farthest into heaven, it is the beating of a loving heart.

HENRY WARD BEECHER

FIVE ESSENTIAL WAYS TO SUPPORT THE BONDING PROCESS.

The following are suggested ways to support bonding using touch, sound and sight. The baby also identifies her mother through smell and taste that naturally occurs during nursing.

1 Touching your baby, skin to skin.

From the moment your baby is born, physical bonding begins through skin-to-skin contact. This creates continuity and security during the baby's first experience of separateness. Touch helps the baby's brain to integrate new nerve impulses and build the capacity to manage the stress of infancy. When parents respond to the cries of their infant with loving touch, the baby learns to gain confidence in how the world responds to its needs.

Suggestion: Put the baby's face against your face and let her rest upon your bare chest. Let the baby sleep on your bare shoulder and in your bare arms.

2 Massaging your baby.

Massage can be used for energizing or calming. Light massage will stimulate the baby's blood flow and aid in circulation. Dr. Frederick Leboyer, the French obstetrician, and author of *Loving Hands—The Traditional Art of Baby Massage* created an innovative program for massaging your baby from head to toe using oils and gentle touch. Leboyer saw that being touched was essential "nutrition" for the baby—as vital as food.

Suggestion: Use gentle repetitive movements by themselves or in combination with soft rocking to nourish your baby's nervous system.

3 Experiencing eye contact with your baby.

During the pregnancy your baby has been listening to you. Now your baby wants to look at you. She wants to know you. You are the person who will love her, care for her, feed her, make her comfortable and help her to grow. Research has shown that newborns learn to recognize their parents' faces within the first days of life and prefer their mother's face to everyone else. They like to look at parents who make direct eye contact, and they turn away when their caregiver is not responsive to them. Gazing into your baby's eyes boosts her brain development and stimulates her to be more awake by raising her heart rate and blood pressure.

Suggestion: Gaze into your baby's eyes and let your baby look directly into your eyes. You will connect at a level that is entrancing and deeply nourishing to both of you.

4 Singing and speaking in a tender way to your baby.

Sound is a vibration that can carry your tender intentions. After birth, newborns will recognize their mother's voice and take great comfort in hearing their parents' voices. Babies respond better to a slower, melodic and repetitive style of speech, which is quite different from regular adult speech. Singing can be especially comforting, particularly if you sang to your baby during pregnancy. As a parent, singing can be a freeing and even joyous experience. Your baby will love it no matter what you sound like!

Suggestion: Babies respond particularly well to voices that use a loving sing-song rhythm. Babies like "play-songs" and lullabies.

5 Playing with your baby.

Play is an important factor in the baby's brain growth. Play stimulates the baby's mind and engages their attention. The baby's brain is immature at birth and goes through rapid sequences of development. As the baby grows out of a newborn state, play becomes another way to bond. Any of the senses can be used in play.

Suggestion: Play a gentle physical game to help your baby feel her body. An interactive poem or a sound and sight activity like "Peek-A-Boo" stimulates you both to laugh.

BONDING IMPACTS YOUR INFANT'S DEVELOPMENT

It has been proven that during the first hours after birth there is a special opportunity for deep bonding to occur between mother and child. Placing the newborn baby directly upon the chest of the mother and maintaining continuous skin-to-skin contact for a period of two to three hours develops a lasting and mutually beneficial connection that is physical, emotional and chemical. This close skin-to-skin contact stimulates the mother's hypothalamus gland to secrete the hormone oxytocin, which is naturally released during childbirth.

Oxytocin, sometimes called the "love hormone," is critical to supporting the process of childbirth.

It induces labor and stimulates the mother's breast milk. It makes the mother and baby slightly sleepy and lessens the mother's physical pain. Oxytocin causes the mother to feel her heart open and calm. It even slows down the mother's blood pressure and heart rate. Oxytocin is also released by the simple action of repetitive and soothing touch of the newborn. This connection, established during nursing, is healthy for both mother and baby. In addition, breast-feeding provides powerful immune support for the baby and initiates many healthy responses in the mother's body.

Though skin-to-skin contact during those first hours is optimal, repeated closeness during the first few months also builds this parent-child bond and has similar impact. Research on mothers and infants show that the babies who experienced this physical and emotional closeness during those first crucial months demonstrated greater adaptability and self-regulation than those who had not. When a baby is self-regulated it means that he is less irritable, less reactive and more alert. The mothers also reported sleeping better and had a deeper sense of well-being.

While bonding is vital to the physical and emotional health and development of the baby, it is equally essential to the self-esteem and confidence of the mother. When a mother bonds with her newborn, it has a positive impact on her hormones, creating the essential chemical and emotional foundation that is critical to attachment.

LISTENING TO YOUR HEART IS THE KEY.

How you connect with your baby establishes the foundation for their capacity for empathy, love, learning and compassion. Your loving words, feelings, and expressions do make a difference. By listening to your heart and your own inner knowing, you are able to access and transmit care and love to your child.

Dr. David says:

FOUR EASY STEPS: CREATING A HEARTFELT CONNECTION

First, if possible, create a place in your home for quiet connection with your baby. Most homes are filled with multiple activities occurring simultaneously. Dedicating a place to nursing and nurturing your baby can enhance a relationship with him.

Second, set up your bonding environment with the necessary equipment. Have a comfortable chair or couch, nursing and feeding supplies, a CD player with remote, the disc and the book, *Safe in the Arms of Love*. Organization can make all the difference in being ready to use your tools.

Third, let others in your home know when you are choosing to have a quiet time. A caregiver's undivided attention has a profound effect on an infant. The normal sound stimuli that exists in most settings is distracting. The music of the CD will support the experience of calm and safety in both of you.

Fourth, cultivate a "practice" with the music daily or as often as possible. Using the music consistently can make it a familiar "friend" and a powerful reminder to connect in a way that is mutually satisfying for the parent and baby.

The "daily practice" is a rich opportunity for connection, exploration and discovery. Use the time to joyfully interact with your baby while listening to the music. Talk to and sing to your baby. Hum along with the music. Try out your own songs. Most of all, stop and enjoy this special time.

Music is Medicine for the Heart

GARY MALKIN

*M*USIC TAKES US ON A JOURNEY. LIKE STORIES, IT CAN TRANS-
port us to places deep within our imagination, to inner landscapes
and places that can touch us only through the magic of sound.
The warm vibration of string, the tender whisper of wind, the gentle pulse of
skin and wood, the incomparable intimacy of the human voice—these aural
textures can take us to new vistas within ourselves. When we visit these lands
and truly listen, allowing the music to touch our
hearts, we can feel refreshed and renewed. When
music is created with the intent to emotionally
touch us, it has the astonishing power to trans-
port us. It infuses us with a sense of peace and
wholeness that feels like home. Music is a miracu-
lous mystery that can soothe us, inspire us, and awaken us into the present
moment, enhancing our lives in significant and inexplicable ways.

*Music is the Sound of
Life, celebrating itself.*

JOHN ORTIZ

Music is everywhere. We take it for granted. We listen while we're driving,
when we're cooking and engaging in the affairs of daily life. We know how
busy our lives can be. Most of us are coming and going at a dizzying pace. It
has become the norm to rush through our days, simultaneously doing many
things at once and inadvertently compromising our sense of well-being.

Singing has been a part of the human experience for as long as we have been on this planet.

Without realizing the ramifications, we allow ourselves to be endlessly available to ever-intruding digital communication devices. Integrating these new gadgets into our lives forces us to significantly alter our lifestyles. Especially when we become parents, the random intrusions can be severe, threatening to undermine our core abilities for focused attention. Imagine how our little ones must feel when we allow ourselves to be chronically distracted. When we deprive ourselves of the rest and quiet we need to function optimally, we cannot give our children the love we feel for them. The cultural epidemic of doing too much and moving too fast continues to adversely affect us all, burrowing its way deep within our nervous systems. It becomes a challenge to remember and protect our ancient, nurturing instincts. These instincts are essential to helping our babies become emotionally and spiritually healthy human beings, ensuring a healthy future for us all.

Thankfully some things never change. Even at a time in which everything seems to be spinning out of control, we can appreciate the simple miracles of life. From the first moment of joy when we learn we are going to have a baby, inherent gifts begin emerging from within and around us. The courage that arises during the birthing process; the wonder of that first moment with your baby; the sensation of nuzzling next to the softest skin in the universe; the realization that you'd risk everything to keep your baby happy, healthy and safe. How can we remember and continue to tap into these simple gifts of life? How can we awaken and maintain our ancient instincts with our profound love intact?

*M*usic has a remarkable power. It can provide a sanctuary in times of challenge and it can serve as a catalyst to align our deepest selves. It is a tool that engages and integrates our hearts, minds, bodies, and souls. Music offers the sublime result of this integration, a state of being that poets refer to as "sudden grace."

Music has the uncanny ability to awaken emotions that change the way we experience life. It creates opportunities to deepen our connection with our loved ones during significant life passages. It can open our hearts so that we can feel things we weren't aware of, causing us to share thoughts and feelings that are often left unsaid. Music anchors our emotions so that we can remember and affirm all that we love.

of where you originate from, all cultures affirm the power of music to move, comfort, and heal our hearts and souls. Recent findings have revealed that the first humans might have been singing long before they actually spoke. Cultural anthropologist Angeles Arrien has often said that the indigenous people of the earth couldn't imagine a day without singing the way we cannot imagine a day without speaking! Singing has been a part of the human experience for as long as we have been on this planet.

*N*ow that a baby has entered your life, take a breath and recognize the great mystery that you are a part of. Let *Safe in the Arms of Love* provide nourishment during this precious time. Soak in these melodies, lyrics, and tender sounds, as you nurse, comfort, talk and sing to your baby. Find your singing voice, no matter what your inner critic might think, and sing as if no one is listening. Open to the experience of gratitude, unconditional love, and appreciation for the miracle of life. When you spend time with your child in this way, I can assure you that a bond will develop that will last forever.

*W*e know listening is the first sense to develop in the womb and the very last sense to leave when we die. We live in a world of sound. Science has shown that everything in the universe is made up of vibrations and frequencies, from the smallest sub-atomic particles to the greatest spheres in the cosmos. When we engage in the experience of sound and music, we are participating in the symphony of life, of which we all are a part.

Listening to music in an intentional way is an effective strategy to deepen and strengthen our connection to our hearts. It is in this spirit that we created *Safe in the Arms of Love*. We prepared every melody, every lyric, and every page to provide a sacred sanctuary for you and your baby.

We've just begun to scratch the surface in understanding the role that music, and especially singing, has played in human cultures. Regardless

The magic of "Musical Medicine" will come into its own. The application of such healing potencies will not be limited just to man's body and mind. It will be an agency for building and healing his soul as well.

CORRINNE HELINE

Dr. David says:

WHAT IS POSITIVE INTENTION MUSIC™?

Over thousands of years, researchers and musicians have discovered the science of sound. Positive Intention Music™ employs psycho-acoustic principles demonstrated to have a specific impact on the nervous system. By intentionally designing the sound, we can shape a listener's experience. As in movies or television, we recall music associated with comedy, drama, action or inspirational moments. The music will have a certain feel that we recognize. This quality derives from the use of tone, tempo and pattern that has an impact on the listener's ear, brain and body.

Parents and newborns are very sensitive to sound. We can support the process of bonding and attachment through the wise use of music. The intentionally designed music of *Safe in the Arms of Love* creates a field of "Positive Emotional Resonance (PER)."

1 With tone, we have utilized instrumentation that minimizes high frequencies, concentrating on midrange tonalities that soothe the nervous system.

2 Tempos are based on the ideal relaxed heartbeat of 50–70 beats per minute.

3 Simple patterns that employ a repetitive melody create easy recognition and memorable tunes. Spacious orchestrations are easily assimilated by the nervous system of both infants and adults.

4 Engaging, intimate lyrics inspire positive feelings and an opening of the heart. The lyrics are specifically written to awaken warm, loving thoughts for babies, that bring peaceful and calm feelings for all.

Experiencing Bonding

WHAT DOES BONDING FEEL LIKE?

ONDING IS AN EXPERIENCE AND A PROCESS. THOUGH IT IS different for everyone, there is a universal quality to bonding that feels warm, loving and kind. Bonding makes you protective. You understand that your baby's needs are more important than your own. A bonded connection feels precious and important. Sometimes, as you are bonding, it feels like you are genuinely shining love from your heart.

Bonding does not happen according to a timetable. Be patient. Some people bond faster than others. In fact, many times the father bonds slower than the mother. It will happen in its own time. If you are having difficulties, talk it over with your health professional.

Bonding creates a strong connection that is stored in both your body and your baby's body. If you experienced bonding with your parents, it is easier to share it with your child. If you did not have a bonded experience when you were a baby, and you do not have those memories stored within you, you can learn what it feels like. The following exercise, Radiating Love, will help those feelings to engage.

> Bonding creates a strong connection that is stored in both your body and your baby's body.

RADIATING LOVE—
A SENSORY EXPERIENCE

The goal of these exercises is to experience a feeling sense of radiance. A feeling sense means that you are remembering something using one or more of your five senses—taste, touch, smell, sight or hearing.

Preparation

To achieve the best results please prepare the following before you begin.

1. **Arrange for ten minutes of uninterrupted time.**

2. **Sit in a comfortable position.**

3. **Plan to use your imagination for learning.**

4. **Learn to breathe a Full Body Breath.**

QUIETING YOUR MIND

Using your imagination requires that you quiet your mind from its normal activity. Often that can be difficult to do. There is so much to think about! When we do quiet the mind, the body is often so tired from the necessities of life that when you relax, it can be easy to fall asleep.

A Full Body Breath will help you to quiet your mind and stay awake. You can use this breath any time you want to relax.

THE FULL BODY BREATH:

Instructions

1. **To begin, breathe in through your nose and exhale through your mouth. Do this a few times to get used to the feeling.**

   If breathing through your nose is not comfortable, breathe in and out through your mouth.

2. **Imagine your body as an expandable balloon that can be filled with air. As you breathe in, let the air expand your chest, your belly and your back.**

   Most adults breathe from their lungs, expanding only their chest. However, breathing deeply into your belly and lower back (around the kidneys) is beneficial for relaxing. Watch your little baby sleeping and you will notice that her body breathes in this way.

3. **As you exhale out of your mouth, let any tension and stress that is in your body easily float out on the air of your exhale.**

   Even if you believe this will only be a temporary relief, do it anyway and feel what happens.

4. **Repeat this a few times until your body feels more relaxed and your mind feels quieter.**

RADIATING LOVE

Please note that there is no right way for this exercise. If you have difficulty you might be trying too hard to do it "right." Sometimes it can take a few attempts to accept that imagination works. It can even be fun.

Instructions

1. Sit comfortably and close your eyes.

2. Imagine you are in a beautiful and relaxing place, feeling the warm light of the sun shining upon your skin.

   This can be a place where you have already been or a place where you would like to be— like resting on a beach or sitting in a beautiful meadow. Choose a place that feels right for you.

3. Inhale with a Full Body Breath as you keep this image in your mind.

4. Feel the warm rays of the sun beaming onto your skin and enjoy this feeling for a few minutes.

   It is not important if your skin actually feels warm. Do not try to make the warmth happen. Simply imagine the sun's warmth shining down onto your skin.

5. Now, change your focus and decide that the sun is in your heart, and feel your heart beaming loving rays moving endlessly outward.

6. Imagine that your baby is lying in your arms or is sleeping in front of you.

   Gently radiate from your chest your loving light to your baby.

7. Imagine your baby loves feeling your loving rays.

8. Take a few minutes and enjoy this experience.

   Some people feel imagined exercises physically. Their skin gets warm. Their breath slows down. Others experience a sense of well-being without "feeling" anything in their body.

A "feeling sense" of radiating love sensitizes you to feeling comfortable with the sensations of bonding.

REVIEWING THE EXPERIENCE

When you know how to send a positive feeling from your heart/chest area, you can recreate that feeling more easily during life's daily challenges.

- When you practice a "feeling sense" choose a simple, accessible image.

- Adding a loving feeling into your imagined scenarios has an effect upon your body and your state of mind.

- Breathing with a Full Body Breath will help you to regain your center.

- If your baby is gassy, fussy or tired, de-stressing with a technique like Full Body Breathe will prove to be invaluable.

- Send gentle rays of love while you talk, sing, rock, and play with your baby. This establishes a quality of connection and security in your child that creates a healthy anchor for you both.

Parents' Stories

First-time Mom

"This is my first child. I expect it will be my only child. I know I worry too much, but with this baby I would swing from excitement to real fear. It was really hard to handle. My friends shared stories with me about their pregnancies and deliveries but frankly no amount of assurance would steady my nerves. I was really afraid that I would not know what to do when things became difficult. I had wanted to be courageous and confident but really my mind kept taking me in a different direction.

The birth went fine. In fact I was thrilled that the birth went so well. But I was certain I was going to make a mistake and somehow harm her. She was so tiny and fragile. She slept for a long time after her birth. She was very quiet, almost as if she were still inside me. My husband was reassuring but I couldn't stop worrying. This was amplified by some of the struggles I had with my initial efforts at nursing.

I was given the *Safe in the Arms of Love* CD by a friend who had just had a baby. She told me she loved the music and that her baby liked it too. I had told her that I was having trouble with nursing. She suggested I nurse with the music to help us to calm down. I asked my husband about it, and he wanted to hear it so we decided to listen to it together. We played the CD as our baby slept and in the middle of the first song I felt my breath slow down. By the second song, my husband and I were holding hands. He really liked all the music, but he especially liked the father song.

After listening to the whole CD, I was amazed that I wasn't feeling any fear. I was much more relaxed and I wanted to be holding my baby. At the next nursing I put the music on again and my daughter was much calmer than usual. It was really sweet. She completed nursing in half the time. I have used it regularly ever since. She loves listening to it, and I use it to put her to sleep. Thank you for creating this wonderful music!"

but I didn't know how much what I do affects my children. Really. It seems so obvious, but one-on-one time, except for story time, was not that important. I just wanted to make sure they were fed, clean and comfortable. I also didn't know how impactful music is for my baby's brain development. I never set up the house to have a quiet time for either baby. It didn't occur to me because I am always multi-tasking and my husband is just like me. So, I decided to try making a special time and place for nursing. It wasn't easy to slow things down and bring the noise level down in the house. I put the music on while his brother was at a play date. I listened without interruptions, not even answering the phone. The impact was immediate.

The music was beautiful and my baby loved it too. When my husband heard it, it really touched him. We now make a point of trying to quiet things down when I am nursing, and when we play with him. The great news is that my three year old loves the music too. Whenever I play it, he quiets down and chills out. It turned out to be a double win!"

Dealing with More than One

"This is my second child. I feel like I was born to be a Mom. I am lucky that I can stay home and not go back to work for a while. Having two little ones is great but it's a lot of work. My older boy just turned three. There haven't been any signs of jealousy, yet. He just wants to hold the baby and be his big brother. He's doing great at it.

I've been pretty tired. My three year old has a lot of energy. He loves to scream and run and especially jump. He's always knocking things over. The only time he likes to sit still is for story time. He really likes that. But, he cries really loud when he gets hurt and it is really hard for him to understand that he has a new little brother who has to sleep.

My friend gave me *Safe in the Arms of Love* as a shower gift but I didn't listen to it 'til after the baby was born. I read the booklet first and I was surprised that much of what I read was actually new to me. I didn't know much about bonding. I never had any trouble loving my sons,

Healing the Battle

"I know this music is powerful because it changed my feelings toward my husband after we had a fight. I wasn't talking to him. We fought about the baby, and how little time we have with each other.

I was still angry when I put on the *Safe in the Arms of Love* music. I don't know what it is about it, but I started crying and feeling really bad that we were fighting. Listening to it just made my heart feel so tender. All I wanted to do was hold the baby and hug my husband. So, I played it for my husband and he had the same reaction. We stopped battling. It just made us appreciate each other more. Thank you. Even the baby loves going to sleep to it."

A Dad Remembering What's Important

"When I heard the music for the first time, I experienced it as deeply nurturing and healing. In addition to tears forming, I had an immediate desire to go home and play with my toddler son. My thought was, "What am I doing here talking about life when I would love nothing more than to be hanging out with my son?" I went home to play with my son. My heart was so open that the quality of the play had more depth than normal. The best way I can explain it is that the love in your music resonated in my body for the longest time.

I received a copy of the CD and I listened attentively. It struck me that I should play this for a woman friend of mine. She is an amazing success story because she grew up in a New Jersey ghetto and had severe deprivation of competent, loving parenting. She especially lacked mothering as an infant and toddler. She has grown into a very caring parent and successful businesswoman but there is still a hole in her soul around bonding and being loved (which she readily recognizes and admits). When I played the CD for her, she started crying . . . not just tearing up but really crying.

Although I know the music is intended for nursing mothers to help with bonding—a purpose that I am confident it will fulfill—I also have experienced it as helpful for all ages in terms of opening the heart and reconnecting with our gentleness. After all, who among us doesn't carry wounds that cannot benefit from a good dose of love and tenderness?"

Dr. David says:

WHAT PARENTS REPORT UPON USING *SAFE IN THE ARMS OF LOVE*

A DEEPER BONDING WITH THEIR BABY— the greatest of joys, appreciation and recognition of the magic that is their baby. Parents feel their hearts more open.

INCREASED CONNECTION WITH ONESELF— feeling more present and focused and able to fully engage "with the moment" and not be distracted by other demands or future concerns.

GREATER SENSE OF INTERNAL RELAXATION— the words, the music and the ritual create a context of relaxation and connection. Parents report feeling more attentive and able to concentrate.

PERCEPTION OF FEELING LESS STRESS— less worry and anxiety about how things are working out since they see, in the moment, that it's working out right there, before their eyes.

Music and rhythm find their way into the secret places of the soul.

PLATO

On Becoming a Mother

LISA RAFEL

It SEEMS SO NATURAL. AFTER ALL, BABIES ARE EVERYWHERE. IT should be easy to adjust and to know what to do when you have a baby.

The first time I really watched a sleeping baby, I was pregnant. I was transfixed by her newborn qualities. She had a look of perfect peace on her delicate face. There was a doll-like quality about her. She was so tiny. When her mother excitedly asked me if I wanted to hold her, I said yes, but I was afraid. The mother put her into my arms and showed me how to support her head. I smiled and acted happy to be holding her, but in actuality, I was very uncomfortable. Holding her did not feel natural to me.

When I reflect back to that moment, I think the reason it did not feel natural to me was because I wasn't captivated with the magic of a baby. Instead, I was thinking about the fear that I was feeling internally. I hadn't considered childbirth as the miracle it is. Those kinds of thoughts never occurred to me.

When I was twenty, I had my first child. She arrived seven weeks early. She was 4 lbs 10 oz., very fragile, and underdeveloped. The incubator became her mother and father. I had a good doctor but in those days doctors didn't know about the importance of bonding. He did not instruct me to touch her and hold her or to come every day and stay with her. Instead he said, "Go home, rest, and build your strength." He assured me that my baby was being well cared for and that after she came home I would be holding her all the time.

At that time, I didn't know about bonding, its importance, or how it occurs. All I knew was that I had given birth to a poorly developed little girl who needed medicine and an incubator. So, I listened to my doctor. I went every day for about an hour to talk to her. The nurse suggested I put my finger into the incubator and stroke the skin on her hand or her cheek. I did that, and then I would go home.

The day my daughter left the hospital, we hired a nurse to help me. She stayed for a few weeks because I was so unsure of what to do. The nurse was confident and she took over. It was easy for her to be with my daughter, but it was not comfortable for me. It felt like she didn't want to be in my arms. Sometimes she would push so hard against me that it was hard to hold on. It was like she was throwing herself out of my arms.

My daughter had many physical problems in the beginning. I wanted to breastfeed but I was told it would be painful and unnecessary for me to pump breast milk while she was in the incubator. When she came home 3 1/2 weeks later, she was still very tiny and allergic to both cow and soy formula. For a long time she had great difficulty holding her food down. In addition, she needed surgery on her eyes, and she had café au lait spots indicating Neurofibromatosis. I was overwhelmed.

My mother and grandmother and her "aunties and uncles" would come by to hold her and play with her and over time she bloomed. I can see now that though I tried to do all the "right things" and I loved my daughter as best I could, my heart had not been tenderized by her presence. In short, we had not bonded.

When I was twenty-two, I gave birth to my son. Though he was three weeks early and also very small, he was able to come home. This time I could nurse and suddenly, without any warning, my heart felt like it was going to burst. I entered into a state of euphoric joy. I was filled with intense feelings of shock and wonder. What a miracle. I knew that I was the source of this child's food and love. My heart was pouring love and through this wave of tenderness, I could feel the magic and wonder of a new soul in my arms.

It makes me sad when I think about my daughter and all that we missed in those first years. However, I have learned that it is never too late to bond. My daughter and I have grown much closer through the years and I am so grateful for the love that has developed between us.

Two years ago I felt an inspiration to create new music. What emerged were beautiful, loving and nurturing songs for expectant and new mothers. It felt like the songs needed to be born and that my heart had helped them come to life. I quickly discovered that everyone who heard the songs said their hearts and minds felt more open and renewed.

The first time I heard Emmy award-winning composer Gary Malkin play the piano, I knew we would work together. By the time I brought him my songs, he had completed *Graceful Passages: A Companion for Living and Dying*, a CD collection of inspiring words and music to ease the dying process. He had been dreaming about working on a project for the beginning of life so the timing was perfect. He immediately wanted to help bring the songs into the world. I am so grateful for this partnership and for his wonderful capacity to make everything so beautiful.

I encourage you to use the lyrics of these songs as examples of what can flow out of your own heart. Speak your heartfelt feelings of love and appreciation to your child—often.

I am grateful to my beloved husband and my loving family—my mother, my children, my stepchildren, our grandchildren and all our friends. Thank you, for the loving support we give to each other.

We do not know how long we will live nor can we predict the circumstances into which we are born. What we can do is to live every day believing that there is a soul in every being and that every soul is important. By doing that, we instantly connect to the source of all of life and we become angels for each other.

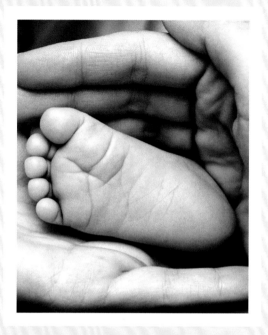

Music is the mediator between the life of the senses and the life of the spirit.

BEETHOVEN

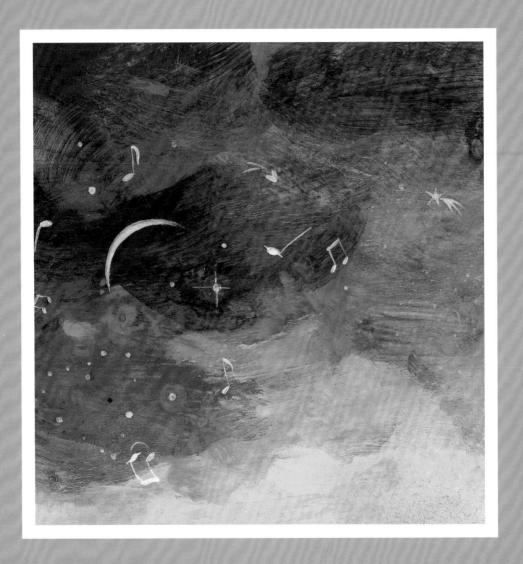

On Becoming a Father

GARY MALKIN

*E*IGHTEEN YEARS AGO, I LEARNED THAT WE WERE EXPECTING. That moment was imprinted on my memory in complete and utter detail: the time of day, where we were, the expression on my wife's face. I remember when I heard that it was 'official', everything changed. Suddenly, I had become aware of a presence that had never existed before. I sensed a glimmer of something entirely new that would ultimately have a significant impact on my life.

Then I realized: I was going to be a father!

From that point on, throughout the pregnancy, all the music that came out of me—everything I composed, everything I played on the piano, every song I sang—became an offering to this new being, a tribute to this miraculous mystery that had entered our lives and who would soon be known as my beloved daughter, Genevieve Rose. Somehow, even when she was as small as a zygote, I sensed that she was deeply listening in rapt attention.

It was when we first saw the blurry images of our child on the sonogram that I started to sing to her, intentionally. I remember snuggling up to my wife's belly, in a prayerful pose, singing to our baby in utero as if I were E.T. phoning home. I did this as many times as my wife would let me, without driving her insane.

By singing to Genevieve early on, I intuitively felt that we might be able to "imprint" her with the voices she would find familiar when she came into this world. I instinctively believed that music—this astonishing language to which I had devoted my entire life—might serve as a kind of rudder for her soul, as it had for me. It was our firm belief that singing and talking to her would build a

healthy "root system" that could support her as she faced our harsh world, with all its challenges and complexities.

For me, singing, creating, and listening to music seemed to be the only way I could come close to the profundity of what was happening to our radically changing little world. We were careening down an unfamiliar river towards parenthood. Without the languages of Love, Music, and Beauty to guide, soothe and hold us, how could we ever prepare for such a metamorphosis in our psyches?

During the months of pregnancy we are given an opportunity to form a strong attachment to our child. By the time our little one comes into the world, we're ready to assume the responsibilities of parenthood. According to the newest brain research, there are few things more important than staying deeply connected to our hearts throughout this process. No matter what our inner or outer life circumstances might be, it's vital to stay in touch with our deep love for our baby. Such steadfast love supports the child's healthy psychological and emotional development. Astonishingly, it can also make the difference between life and death, as I soon found out.

Our pregnancy proceeded smoothly, without any indication of the challenges that lay ahead. But as often happens in life, things took a turn that we never could have anticipated. We had a very difficult birth.

My wife endured Herculean, life-threatening challenges during her thirty-five hours of labor. Our precious baby, struggling for her life as well, had to be rushed to the Neonatal Intensive Care Unit moments after her birth.

During those tense hours, as my wife was receiving medical attention, we didn't know if our precious child would survive. I remained by Genevieve's side as I watched her shaking from the trauma of entering the world in this way. Tubes were attached to seemingly every part of her tiny body as she rested in her little bed. I gently placed my left hand on the top of her tiny head, and put my right hand's pinky finger out for her to grasp.

*M*y tiny child, literally minutes old, grabbed onto my finger and wouldn't let go. Time seemed to stop in mid-air. I sang to her. I whispered to her. I told her how much we loved her, how much we're looking forward to getting to know her, how much we couldn't wait to watch her grow. I don't know how many hours passed in this way.

Suddenly I saw a marked change in the color of her skin. It turned from pale grey to a beautiful, bright pink. Seeing this change, the nurse gave me an assuring, comforting smile. Our beloved daughter had finally turned a corner.

I found myself taking a deep breath for the first time in hours. Genny was going to make it. I felt certain that the relationship we had formed during all those times we sang and spoke to her before she was born had somehow helped her to grab onto life, as firmly as she had grasped my little finger.

The birth process asks us to stretch our hearts wider than they have ever been stretched before. I learned that bringing a new life into this world is as primal as anything I would ever know. It took us to the very depths of our abilities to be present, to love and care for one another, and to be all that we can be.

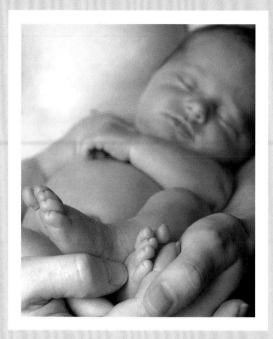

Going through this life-altering experience left us deeply exhausted. When we were finally able to come home, we constantly played background music as a way to keep our hearts open and soothe our shattered nerves. The music told us—as only music can—that with time, all would be well.

Throughout those tender months, especially during the hours of nursing, soothing music continually filled our home. I remember those days and nights as luminous and precious, feeling gratitude beyond imagining.

Ever since then, I had often dreamed of creating something that could serve both parent and child during that special time after birth. I wanted to create something that would affirm the healing power of unconditional love, no matter what the birth experience was.

When my friend Lisa Rafel invited me to collaborate on this work with her, I jumped at the opportunity. And these songs! Like beautiful gemstones, one by one she brought forward these inspired, touching songs that held within them so much innocence, wisdom, and tenderness. These were not just songs, but a kind of medicine music for the heart, designed for a time when we are most transparent and intimate with life.

The great portals at the beginning and end of life require wisdom, compassion, and tenderness. How we behave during these life passages defines what we value most in our lives. If we can use the gift of music to soothe, deepen, and connect us during these important times, our lives and the lives of those around us might be more loving and meaningful. Listen to this music with your heart and your whole being. If you let yourself bathe in this experience, you will be nourished.

The journey of parenting our daughter from the moment she was born has molded me into the man I have now become. I've learned that there is nothing more important than devoting yourself to the love you have for your child. While life will always have challenges, you can make no wiser choice than taking the time to establish this one-of-a-kind loving connection. This primal love is the epicenter of your connection with the Source of Life itself. By nurturing this connection of unconditional love, you can expand the muscle that never ceases growing—your miraculous heart. After all, there's only one force that matters in this life, the one we take with us when we die—Love.

I am deeply grateful to Lisa for bringing these songs forth and for allowing me to help bring them to life. I am grateful for the warm and empowering partnership I've enjoyed with David Surrenda during every phase of this project. He always is a continual font of insight, ideas, and support. Thanks to our sound engineer, Howard Johnston, for his incredible talent to capture the heart of the sound. Deep thanks to the dedicated singers and musicians, without whom this work would never have become a musical source of tenderness and love.

May this music remind you, like a dream, of when you were a newborn yourself. Allow it to rock you into a remembrance of what we all are in this life, *Safe, in the Arms of Love.*

Among the Pueblos of New Mexico, part of the childbirth ritual requires that the woman who delivers the baby greets the infant with a song.

MITCHELL GAYNOR, M.D.

Afterword

JOEL EVANS, M.D.

*A*FTER LISTENING QUIETLY TO *SAFE IN THE ARMS OF LOVE*, I realized that it was the perfect title for this musical resource that was created to enhance that essential early bond between parent and child. Listening to this beautiful music supports the parents' natural ability to provide their newborn a sense of connection and safety—exactly what their baby needs as it transitions into this world.

There is a pivotal point when a baby must separate from the magical place from which it has grown. Many believe that this magic kingdom—the sanctuary of a mother's womb—is infused with a connection to the Divine, providing a quality of wholeness that cannot be found in this world. However, the child must ultimately endure a profound separation from that wholeness upon birth. Making that separation as easy as possible is critical for the healthy development of your child.

Babies have needs and wants, as well as thoughts and feelings, from the instant of birth. Growing evidence suggests that long before birth, there is a consciousness that exists while the baby is in the womb. Given this strong possibility, it is vital for the mother to do whatever she can do to maintain a peaceful and loving experience for her and her baby, both during pregnancy and during the early days and months after birth.

The wonder of *Safe in the Arms of Love* lies in its innocence and its accessibility at a time when those qualities are needed most. Whenever it is that your baby develops its consciousness, if you allow yourself to listen and be swept away by this music, *Safe in the Arms of Love* will support you and your baby to feel safe and loved during this crucial time of development.

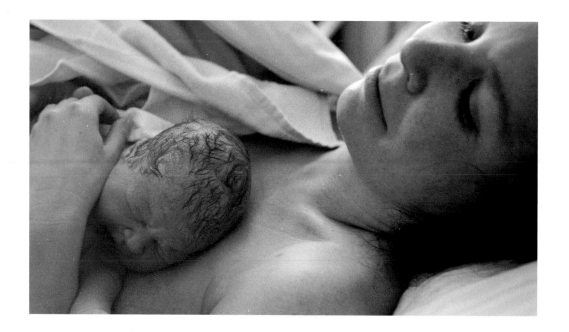

eeling welcome and wanted is a prerequisite for a newborn—or preborn—to feel comfortable as the baby gets accustomed to its new environment. By knowing and experiencing unconditional love, a newborn develops a sense of self that is filled with confidence instead of fear, doubt and insecurity. This is important because being loved serves as the strongest lesson in how to love, leading to strong, fulfilling, and healthy interpersonal relationships. Finally, feeling heard and paid attention to from the very beginning, can prevent feelings of rejection or being unseen, experiences that often result in disruptive and aggressive behaviors that are used to attract attention.

n making your child feel wanted and loved, especially from the very beginning, you will begin to realize that, in a very real sense, the greatest gift you can give yourself and your baby is a consistent, ongoing experience of deep love, peace and connection.

How does *Safe in the Arms of Love* enhance this experience for you and your baby? How can listening and participating with music or tenderly singing songs impact the emotional experience during the bonding process? Research has shown that babies can hear while in the womb, and it is important to note that changes in babies' bodily functions have been documented when songs that they've heard in utero were sung to them after birth. Science has also shown that newborns sensitively absorb the thoughts and feelings of their parents during the bonding process. Whether you are pregnant or you have a new baby, focused listening to *Safe in the Arms of Love*, and singing and speaking along with the music, will create a joyful context within which those important messages of love and acceptance can enter your child's subconscious mind, creating what all parents want for their children: a healthy sense of self that will last a lifetime.

DR. EVANS is the author of *The Whole Pregnancy Handbook—An Obstetrician's Guide to Integrating Conventional and Alternative Medicine Before, During and After Pregnancy*. The book is a resource designed for healthcare professionals, pregnant women and their supportive partners.

To stop the flow of music would be like the stopping of time itself, incredible and inconceivable.

AARON COPELAND

8 Themes to Remember

1 Bonding is a universal human experience that is vital to the future well-being of your baby. Allow yourself to know and experience the five ways you can bond with your baby.

2 Music is a powerful way to support your emotional connection with another being. Music can be medicine for the heart. It can awaken us to a new level of emotional aliveness.

3 Positive Intention Music™ (psycho-acoustically designed) can affect your physiology and emotions. It can support an experience of opening the heart and build connectivity and resonance between you and your child.

4 Be present with your baby. Take the time to listen to and really HEAR the music as you nurse or play.

5 Design your home environment to make it easy to succeed by creating a quiet space to connect with your baby.

6 Make listening to the music a whole family experience. As often as you can, include your partner and other children (if you have them) into appreciating a shared listening space.

7 Enjoy feeling the resonance grow between you and your baby as you continue to tune in to each other through activities and music.

8 Radiate your love to your baby. Remember that a happy home is all about connection and love. Discover how you can develop your own unique ways of expressing love with your child.

Your child has a unique personality filled with distinctive gifts. Let go of being busy and find quiet time to receive the signals your child is giving you.

Safe *in the* Arms *of* Love

The Lyrics

Music is the language of the spirit. It opens the secret of life bringing peace, abolishing strife.
KAHLIL GIBRAN

Always in Your Heart

Rest your head, go to sleep—Let your dreams fall away
Drop into the silent deep—Where your soul can play

Breathe your breath with my breath—Rocking, like the ocean floor
Love is like nothing else—Always there—more in store

I love you near or far—it doesn't matter where you are
Even apart, we're always touching hearts—Always touching hearts

My love is strong as the wind—And as wide as the sky
It's filled with joy—can you feel it?—So soft, like a butterfly

Rest your head on my heart, Feel what's coming to you
It's my glow, now you know—How love feels when it's true

Sleep my sweet wild rose—Gather strength like the sea
Your smile is bright as a rainbow—A light for all to see

Hear this prayer I sing to you—Know that when we're apart,
I am always with you—I'm there, deep in your heart.

Even when we're apart, I am always in your heart

Angel of the Cosmos

Good night, sweet child—Sleep and dream in peace
What a gift you are—You've come from so far away

Good night, sweet one—A blessing from the stars
Welcome home, our little one—Into loving arms

Good night, sweet face—Let your body rest
Like a small cocoon—Sleeping on my chest

Good night, sweet pea—Let the dreaming start
See the place you came from—In our loving hearts

Soft, sweet—Let your eyelids close
We are here beside you, to wrap you in our love

Soft, sweet—Gentle heart and soul
Angel of the Cosmos—We wrap you in our love

Dream deep, sleep, sleep—We know who you are
Like a gift from Heaven—A light born from the stars

Sleep, sleep sweet dreams—All throughout the night
Loving you is easy—You're beauty filled with light.

Loving you is easy—You're beauty filled with light.

Safe, in the Arms of Love

Sweet face, so soft—Like an Angel, we know
You will sleep well tonight
Soundly, gently—Little lights lifting you
Taking you into flight

Gentle whispers—Everyone marveling
Sounds of love above
We are beaming—Feel our hearts holding you
Rocking you, tender with love

Oh radiant child—A lamp for the world
Your eyes so bright and clear
We are so blessed to receive you
Precious one, we are near

Dearest baby—Angels are watching you
Always there, above
Sleep now, sweet dreams—Feel our hearts holding you
Safe, in the arms of love

We are so blessed to receive you
Precious one—We are here

Dearest baby—Angels are watching you
Always there, above

Sleep now, sweet dreams—Feel our hearts holding you
Safe, in the arms of love

For the Rest of Our Lives

I can't believe you're here—
The way you fit inside my hands
How you turn to hear my voice
Like you know who I am

Your tiny fingers grab my thumb
The softness of your cheek
Your eyes unlock my heart
This love's so sweet

In this tender hour—
I can feel it in my bones
There's a love growing tonight
From a bond so deep inside
I will carry your heart in mine
For the rest of our lives

This morning when you cried
I felt helpless inside—
I thought to run away
But I opened up my mind

'Cause you're a part of me,
Like a branch of a tree
When I look into your face,
I see the wonder and grace of
    what can be.

In this precious hour—sweet baby
    child of mine
There's a love growing tonight

From a bond so deep inside
I'll carry your heart in mine
For the rest of our lives

These feelings are so soft
I won't let them fade away
You're a flower in my hands
Blooming every day
Like the wind can wake the sea
You'll be always changing me
I will protect this place
Of grace and love and faith in
    you and me

In this bonding hour—I feel it in my
    bones
There's a love growing tonight
From a place so deep inside
I will carry your heart in mine
For the rest of our lives

This will grow—If I will cherish what
    you do
Hmmm, I will shine my love on you
Every day, every day, like morning dew
I will love you—Yes, I will—love you.

Song for the Ancestors

Close your eyes, let them fall—Into Sleep
Breathe your breath, like a song—So complete
Ancestors, from above—Are watching you
Sending love, like angel dust—To comfort you

Breathe and sigh, dreams will fly—To where they are
Gone yet near, so wise and clear—Hear their song
They are watching over you—From above
Feel their strength guiding you—With pure love

In your body is their code that makes you grow
Precious gifts inside you, protect you and guide you
In your sleep they kiss your cheek and brush your tears away
"We are here, in your heart, always near."

Sleep and dream my little one—Take your time
Breathe your breath, like a song—It's yours to chime
Your Ancient ones will come to you—From above
Feel their strength guiding you—With pure love

In your sleep they kiss your cheek and brush your tears away
Ancient lights, shine with love, to help you on your way.

Biographies

LISA RAFEL

Lisa Rafel creates songs and teaching programs to help people experience greater joy and connection. She is a teacher, "sound healing" educator, song-writer and singer, as well as an internationally recognized spiritual teacher, author, poet, and recording artist with numerous CD's.

Lisa founded **Resonant Sounds, LLC** to support the connection between new parents and their babies through the use of intentional music. She is dedicated to creating music, books and applications that support that intimate connection. Her understanding of psycho-acoustic principles and the importance of engaging music, combined with the power of intentional language comes from a long career in the theater arts, sound healing, poetry and the use of the voice. She writes her music from the heart of a loving mother and grandmother. Lisa has two children and six grandchildren.

Lisa's teaching is grounded in her deep understanding of the importance of conscious transitions and courageous compassion. Her *Resonate With The Soul*™ programs include transformative and self-healing techniques using modern scientific principles mixed with practices from ancient and indigenous cultures. She teaches Vocal Sound Healing programs for individuals and groups internationally and uses creative cross-disciplinary techniques in her work with adults and children.

She is a founding board member of the Sound and Music Alliance (SAMA).

More about Lisa Rafel's teaching programs can be found at www.lisarafel.com.

GARY MALKIN

Gary Malkin is an Emmy award-winning composer, producer, performer, and public speaker dedicated to making a difference in the world by creating musical resources and events that inspire the heart and catalyze societal and individual healing. As the composer of numerous award-winning television and film projects for nearly thirty years, Gary is known for working on socially responsible media projects featuring themes such as the environment, tolerance, children's welfare, cancer, and global healing.

Gary is passionate about the universal role music (and all the arts) can play as a catalyst for a more inclusive spirituality. He is the co-creator of the acclaimed CD/gift book, *Graceful Passages*, released by his life-enhancing media production company, Wisdom of the World, which offers aesthetic ways to directly experience the world's known and unknown visionaries to help us face our life transitions with more mindfulness, presence, and compassion.

He has served as the Artistic Director for the Quest for Global Healing international conferences, (which featured Archbishop Desmond Tutu, among other Nobel Laureates) and performed on the stage of the Great Hall of China, featuring the power of music as a healing resource. An in-demand public speaker, he has presented at places such as Harvard's Conference on Spirituality and Health, Scripps Clinic, and UCSF Medical School. Through everything he does, Gary is dedicated to using music and media as a resource to help us to deepen our lives with a greater connection to who we are and what matters most. He is the proud father of his daughter, Genevieve Rose, who, along with his ex-wife, Suzanne, has taught him everything he knows about what it means to serve and love another unconditionally.

DAVID SHEPPARD SURRENDA, Ph.D.

Dr. David Surrenda, a licensed clinical psychologist, has conducted executive level organizational consultation and coaching with business, government, education and health systems for 35 years. He has worked extensively with hospitals and national health systems to support innovations, solutions and new paradigmatic thinking. He is currently the CEO of Kripalu Center for Yoga and Health, a retreat and research center in Stockbridge Massachusetts.

Dr. Surrenda was the founder, Dean and curriculum director for the Graduate School of Holistic Studies at John F. Kennedy University for nine years. He crafted the first nationally accredited graduate program in Holistic Health Education, a forerunner to the current efforts in Integrative Health. He currently sits on the Boards of two health foundations (Fannie E. Rippel Foundation and the Bravewell Collaborative). These foundations are committed to the radical improvement of the American health system through integrative thinking, seeding innovation and convening key influencers to dialogue and consider how to drive sustainable system change.

As a clinician, David helped pregnant couples and families to address the issues that arise during major life transitions.

He is the author of three books. His most recent is *Retooling on the Run: Real Change for Leaders with No Time*, (co-authored with Stuart Heller), a unique roadmap for cultivating versatility of leadership action styles. He also served for six years as the co-CEO of a training and research corporation, developing nationally recognized innovations in conflict resolution and crisis intervention.

David is the proud father of three daughters and has six grandchildren.

Credits

All Songs* Composed by Lisa Rafel
Music Produced and Arranged by Gary Malkin
   *except for: *Song of the Ancestors* and
   Safe in the Arms of Love
Lyrics by Lisa Rafel, Music by Lisa Rafel and Gary Malkin
Engineered and Mixed by Howard Johnston
Assistant Engineered by Tyler Crowder
Keyboard Sweetening by Dan Alvarez
Mastered by Ira Ingber at Muscletone Studio West,
   Los Angeles, CA
All live music tracks recorded at Fantasy Studios, Berkeley, CA
All programming and sweetening tracks recorded at
Wisdom of the World Studios, San Francisco, CA

1) *Always in Your Heart* (6:22)

Music and Lyrics by Lisa Rafel
Lisa Rafel, Lead Vocal
Kris Yenney, Cello
Natalie Cox, Harp
Gary Malkin, Piano
Matt Eakle, Flute
Julia Quinn, Gabrielle Quinn, and Ian Quinn, Background Vocals
Gary Malkin & Dan Alvarez, Keyboard Sweetening

2) *Time to Be* (1:23)

Music by Gary Malkin
Gary Malkin, Piano
Matt Eakle, Flute

3) *Angel of the Cosmos* (4:31)

Music and Lyrics by Lisa Rafel
Linda Tillery, Lead Vocal
Kris Yenney, Cello
Gary Malkin, Piano
Gary Malkin & Dan Alvarez, Keyboards

4) *Sanctuary* (1:12)

Music by Lisa Rafel and Gary Malkin
Sandy Griffiths, Vocals
Gary Malkin & Dan Alvarez, Keyboards

5) *Embrace* (1:34)

Music by Gary Malkin
Gary Malkin, Piano
Gary Malkin & Dan Alvarez, Keyboards

6) *Safe in the Arms of Love* (5:44)

Lyrics by Lisa Rafel
Music by Lisa Rafel and Gary Malkin
Evelie Delfino Sales Posch, Lead Vocal
Natalie Cox, Harp
Kris Yenney, Cello
Gary Malkin, Piano
Annie Stocking, Background Vocals
Sandy Griffiths, Background Vocals
Sandy Cressman, Background Vocals
Gary Malkin & Dan Alvarez, Keyboards

7) *The Rest of Our Lives* (6:59)

Music and Lyrics by Lisa Rafel
Skyler Jett, Lead Vocal
Tal Morris, Acoustic Guitar
Gary Potterton, Acoustic Guitar
Tom Corwin, Bass
Gary Malkin & Dan Alvarez, Keyboards

8) *Reverie* (:55)

Music by Gary Malkin
Gary Malkin, Piano
Gary Malkin & Dan Alvarez, Keyboards

9) *Song of the Ancestors* (4:11)

Lyrics by Lisa Rafel
Music by Lisa Rafel and Gary Malkin
Christina Quinn, Lead Vocal
Gary Malkin, Piano
Annie Stocking, Background Vocals
Sandy Griffiths, Background Vocals
Sandy Cressman, Background Vocals
Gary Malkin & Dan Alvarez, Keyboards

10) *Coming Home* (4:14)

Music by Gary Malkin
Gary Malkin, Piano
Matt Eakle, Flute
Jeremy Cohen, Violin
Gary Malkin & Dan Alvarez, Keyboards

All songs published by Nanalisa Music, (ASCAP)
except: *Time to Be*; *Embrace*; *Reverie*; *Coming
Home*; Published by Furniture Music, (ASCAP).

Acknowledgements

In the past half-century, a fundamental change has occurred in the area of infant behavior, child development, bonding and attachment. This shift in the quality of the dialogue and in the quantity of research is the result of the pioneering efforts, persistence and passion of a small group of researchers, thinkers and writers. These individuals courageously raised difficult questions and challenged accepted points of view. They offered alternative approaches and committed to conversing about controversial issues with the leading professionals in their field.

We gratefully acknowledge them, for without their work, our efforts would not be entering as rich and vital a field. We thank them for their commitment and fortitude. Their explorations have revealed essential information regarding the relationship between birth and quality of family and community. There is still much before us to discover and we are honored to be a part of this journey. We recognize John Bowlby, Mary Ainsworth, Mary Main, Marshall and Phyllis Klaus, John Kennell, T. Berry Brazelton, William and Martha Sears, Magda Gerber, Urie Bronfenbrenner, Erik Erikson, Frederick Leboyer, and Benjamin Spock. They have taught us the importance of being aware of both how to raise infants and how to bring them into the world.

We honor the modern pioneers who courageously brought to light new ways to integrate ancient sound and music with the wisdom of science. We are grateful to the first singers and music makers who carried this primal language throughout the ages. It is also important for us to honor the source of sound, that "big bang" that brought us into existence. This core vibration is the common denominator of the cosmos.

In keeping with honoring the music makers, we would like to thank our additional lead vocalists whose beautiful performances celebrate our universal love of children.

Skyler Jett	Evelie Posch	Christina Quinn	Linda Tillery

Thank you to our families who have inspired us.

Lisa, Gary and David

RESONANT SOUNDS

Resonant Sounds, LLC is dedicated to helping parents experience healthy bonding with their baby. We create musical environments, products and tools that support intimate, healthy and heartfelt connections.

Bonding with our babies is vital to their physical health and psychological well-being. Our technologically influenced culture bombards us with overstimulation and constant distraction, compromising the time for essential parent-child connection. We recognize that the failure to form healthy attachments with primary caregivers affects a baby's long-term capacity for relationship, security, trust, communication, confidence and compassion.

Resonant Sounds is creating a family of products that utilize Positive Intention Music™ (PIM) to facilitate parent-child bonding during both the critical initial periods of an infant's life as well as during the last trimester in utero. Positive Intention Music™ employs the psycho-acoustic principles of rhythm, tempo and pitch to create specific positive physiological responses in the listener.

Accompanying the music, we produce easy to read, beautiful, information-rich books filled with current research about the importance of bonding, effective ways to connect with your infant, personal bonding stories, poetry and methods to de-stress.

Our first product, *Safe in the Arms of Love*, a book and music set, serves the needs of the newborn and supports the parent to relax into an experience that naturally strengthens the bonding process. The music establishes a deep sense of connection and unconditional love between parent and child.

Our second book and music set, *Safe in the Womb of Love*, addresses how parents can connect with their baby while in utero. The beautiful music evokes the expectations and hopes of parenthood. The book offers practical advice and exercises for parents and includes the five essential bonding processes that support the healthiest family birth experience (to be released in late 2011).

Additional products will include music/book sets, children's books, toys, and nurturing travel supplies for babies. We are also designing products that can be utilized with infants in the hospital.

Resonant Sounds gives presentations and workshops for pregnant families on the skills and perspectives associated with healthy bonding.

To learn more, please see our website: **www.resonantsounds.com,** or call **415-968-5600.**

A portion of the proceeds from Resonant Sounds sales goes to support charities that help build a safe and joyful connection between parents and their children.

WISDOM OF THE WORLD
Media for a Meaningful Life

Wisdom of the World is a global media publishing company, creating products that deeply touch people's lives. We deliver the spoken wisdom of known and unknown visionaries of our time, enhanced with music and powerful imagery. Our innovative tools cultivate spiritual and emotional intelligence, empowering people to access and share their innate wisdom and realize a greater sense of meaning in their lives.

We use the power of music to deliver visceral experiences of integrity and intimacy. We are dedicated to cultivating integration, wholeness, and presence, offering experiences that heal, empower, and connect us to the very best part of ourselves.

Through our *WisdomTraks*, *WisdomFilms*, and *Sound Sanctuaries*, as well as through our presentations, performances and workshops, our goal is to help people:

Remember and connect to their true purpose

Cultivate radical gratitude

Create healing environments through the power of music

Strengthen their capacity for compassionate relationships

Deepen their ability to live life with an open heart

Contact us to learn more about our "alchemized wisdom" recordings (spoken wisdom with music), our sound sanctuaries (instrumental music) or our vocal music. We invite you to subscribe to our e-newsletter of events and new recordings, join our community or to inquire about our keynote presentations, performances, and workshops. For this and more, go to **www.wisdomoftheworld.com.**

WISDOM OF THE WORLD
336 Bon Air Center #143, Greenbrae, CA 94904
Toll Free: 888-242-6608, Fax: 415-461-2882
www.wisdomoftheworld.com

Wise Parenting Press

P.O. Box 20836, Piedmont, CA 94611

www.wiseparentingpress.com

COVER & BOOK DESIGN by Jennifer Durrant / jenniferdurrantdesign.com

ILLUSTRATION by Anne Kristin Hagesaether/eastwing.co.uk

EDITED by Shoshana Alexander

Distribution to trade bookstores in the U.S. and Canada:

PUBLISHERS GROUP WEST

1700 Fourth Street

Berkeley, CA 94710

PHONE: 800-788-3123 FAX: 800-351-5073

For individual orders:

WISE PARENTING PRESS

P.O. Box 492

Stockbridge, MA 01262

PHONE: 415-968-5600

www.wiseparentingpress.com

Library of Congress Cataloging-in-Publication Data available

ISBN: 978-0-615-35994-6

10 9 8 7 6 5 4 3 2 1

Printed in China by Palace Press International

  Palace Press International, in association with Roots of Peace, will plant two trees for each tree used in the manufacturing of this book. Roots of Peace is an internationally renowned humanitarian organization dedicated to eradicating land mines worldwide and converting war—torn lands into productive farms and wildlife habitats. Together, we will plant two million fruit and nut trees in Afghanistan and provide farmers there with the skills and support necessary for sustainable land use.

MEDICAL DISCLAIMER

This book is not intended as a substitute for medical advice. The reader should regularly consult with a physician or a healthcare professional in matters relating to health and particularly in respect to any symptoms that may require diagnosis or medical attention.